HELEN KELLER

A Life From Beginning to End

Copyright © 2018 by Hourly History.

Table of Contents

Introduction

Most stories about Helen Keller focus on the things that made her different from many of us. They tell about her unique childhood, about the remarkable ways in which she experienced the world, and about her courage in overcoming the exceptional difficulties of her life. These stories often stop short just when Keller entered adulthood, having published her own early autobiography and earned her college degree. Although these tales are certainly fascinating and inspiring, they are also incomplete.

Helen Keller was more than an encouraging story about overcoming handicaps, more than a poster child for the education of the deafblind. The intelligence and determination that gave Keller the distinction of being the first deafblind person to earn a bachelor's degree carried her past that degree and into an active, opinionated life. Sometimes the opinions that she expressed may clash with the ideas of many of the people who are motivated by Keller's early experiences, but they are nonetheless a part of her true story.

Helen Keller's story is of someone who, like the rest of us, was nothing less than a complicated, inimitable human being.

Chapter One

Growing up Deaf and Blind at Ivy Green

"What we have once enjoyed we can never lose. All that we love deeply becomes a part of us."

—Helen Keller

Pure joy had come to the little cottage draped with roses and honeysuckle in Tuscumbia, Alabama. According to Southern custom, Arthur Henley Keller, newspaper editor and former Confederate officer, had built a small house beside Ivy Green, his modest family homestead. When Arthur married his second young wife, Catherine "Kate" Everett Adams, they moved into the cottage together. Now, on June 27, 1880, a little girl joined Arthur and Kate in their one-room hideaway.

Arthur couldn't remember what the tiny child's name was to be; he had disagreed with Kate about which relative's name their firstborn should carry, so when he arrived at the church and the minister asked him to state the name of his daughter, Arthur did his best. He gave the name of his mother-in-law; the baby would be called Helen Adams Keller.

The beauties of green fields, blue skies, and a tree-shaded flower garden etched themselves into the soul of tiny Helen, never to be forgotten. She began learning to talk—she could soon say "water"—and on her first birthday she made her first trying steps across the room to join the play of sunshine and shadows on the cottage floor. That initial attempt at walking ended in a tumble and tears, a misfortune shared by all beginning adventurers, but before the baby reached her second birthday, an unthinkable tragedy altered her life experiences forever. Helen became dangerously ill in February of 1882, perhaps with scarlet fever or meningitis. The doctor was delighted when the fever suddenly disappeared, and the child who had been so near death began to recover.

But little Helen no longer chased after splashes of sunshine. When she was well enough to get out of bed, she clung desperately to her mother's dress. She could still recognize her mother by the touch of her hands, but she could not see her. For some time, Helen continued to pronounce words such as "water," but she could no longer hear the sounds made by her lips. With horror, the Keller family came to realize that their precious baby had become both blind and deaf.

Although she was trapped in a world of absolute silence and darkness, Helen grew and learned like any other child. Kate permitted her daughter's curious fingers to run over every object and action in their home, and Helen communicated very effectively by mimicking the actions she could feel others performing. In turn, by feeling the actions that her mother signed to her, Helen could even be sent on errands to fetch things in the house. At five years old, she could help out with family chores by folding and putting away the clean laundry, recognizing the clothing by touch. She could play in the garden, touching and smelling the abundant flowers, whose bright colors she could still remember.

Helen had a playmate in Martha Washington, the cook's daughter. Helen could feel, smell, and taste the delights of the kitchen house, where the two little girls helped to knead dough, make homemade ice cream, and grind coffee. In spite of her handicaps, Helen was a strong-willed child and the leader of the two. When the girls went hunting for guinea eggs in the tall grass, Helen always insisted on carrying their treasures home. In spite of the fact that she was blind, Helen was certain that she could carry the eggs more safely than Martha, who might fall and drop them.

Though Helen's curious fingers could help in the kitchen, learn about milking cows, torment the dog, and get into mischief—such as using scissors to cut off most of Martha's hair—they could not teach her about concepts that only language could communicate. Helen could help to prepare Christmas goodies and hang up her own stocking, but she could not understand the Christmas story nor share in the anticipation of Christmas morning.

As Helen grew older, her intelligence and need for self-expression developed. She was also physically healthy, very robust, strong, and active. She had an indisputably lovely face with golden curls and blue eyes. Her left eye was distinctly larger than the other, however, causing photographers who wished to represent her at her best to take her pictures only in profile.

Helen had developed more than 60 signs with which to communicate with others, but at some point, her fingers taught her that other people used their mouths to talk with one another. As she slowly realized that her life was more constricted than that of those around her, anger and frustration often erupted in screams, flailing, hitting, and kicking. When she learned how to use a key, she locked her mother into the pantry and then sat with her back to the door to relish the jarring sensation of her mother's pounding, well aware of how naughty she was being.

In 1886, a little sister named Mildred came to join Helen and her two older half-brothers, all of whom now lived together in the bigger home. When Helen wanted to crawl into her mother's lap, her fingers felt the infant there, and she was rejected. Naturally, Helen had no love for the trespasser, and at times her selfish fury made her dangerous to the baby.

The older she became, the more Helen instinctively wanted to expand her knowledge and capabilities, but her handicaps prohibited her from discovering and expressing things like other children. Her terrible fits of frustration became a daily—and sometimes an hourly—occurrence, whenever someone failed to understand her signs or allow her to have her own way. These outbursts of rage and irritation left Helen sobbing and exhausted, feeling trapped by the unremitting silence and darkness, unable to form her thoughts into words even in her own mind, since language was unknown to her.

Constantly restless, endlessly investigating her surroundings, Helen was destructive simply because she did not have enough constructive outlets for her energies. Whatever she demanded was instantly given to her by her compassionate family, making Helen an unmanageable, violent, manipulative child who was quickly becoming impossible to live with.

When she was six years old, Helen's parents took her to Baltimore by train to see an eye specialist. Helen enjoyed the trip, on which she strung a box of shells given to her by a fellow passenger and played with the conductor's ticket punch, but the results were disappointing. Nothing could be done for Helen's eyes. Only education could relieve her imprisoned existence.

The eye specialist sent Helen's father to Washington in July of 1886 to see Alexander Graham Bell, the famous inventor of the telephone. Bell was well-known for his work with the deaf. He was able to understand the things that Helen signed to him, and more importantly, he gave hope to her family. Bell directed the Keller family to Perkins Institute for the Blind in Boston. A letter was sent to the institute, and a teacher was promised for little Helen.

On March 3, 1887, Miss Anne Mansfield Sullivan arrived at Ivy Green.

Chapter Two

Water for a Thirsty Soul

"The best and most beautiful things in the world cannot be seen or even touched. They must be felt with the heart."

—Helen Keller

Fifty years before Anne Sullivan found little Helen Keller on the porch of Ivy Green, Dr. Samuel Howe had invented a method whereby he taught another blind and deaf girl, Laura Bridgman, how to read and write, thereby unlocking the world around a deafblind person through the gift of language for the very first time. Anne Sullivan, who suffered from limited eyesight herself, had attended the Perkins Institute for the Blind and learned from Laura Bridgeman the method of signing the letters of the alphabet into the hands of the deafblind.

Only 20 years old, Anne Sullivan had a high sense of purpose for her life. At her graduation from Perkins Institute, she had admonished her friends that "duty bids us go forth into active life. Let us go cheerfully, hopefully, and earnestly, and set ourselves to find our especial part. When we have found it, willingly and faithfully perform it."

The morning after her arrival, Anne led her small pupil into the bedroom that had been assigned to her. She had a gift and a first lesson for the little girl; she placed a new doll into the child's arms and signed the letters for "doll" into her hand. Helen could not be told that Laura Bridgman had made the doll's clothes and dressed it for her or that Anne had come to teach her to understand words. She felt the strange signs that Anne made on her hands, but she did not comprehend them. She was certainly intelligent enough, however, to rapidly learn to mimic the unfamiliar signs after an initial battle of wills between the new teacher and pupil.

Anne's patience and ingenuity were sorely tried during the following days as Helen made no real connection between the objects around her and the words that Anne attempted to teach her. Instead, the little girl repeatedly demonstrated that she was as obstinate and willful as any child who has not had the advantage of loving discipline. Helen's family, pitying her handicaps, had not known how to control her rages. Anne, firmly believing in the child's ability to develop her capabilities, was determined to conquer her limitations.

At the table, Helen not only ate with her fingers but freely put her hands into the serving dishes and other people's plates as well. When Anne tried to curb this behavior, Helen threw herself to the floor and began to scream and thrash. Upset, the rest of the family exited the room, leaving Helen alone with her teacher. Anne locked the door and continued to eat. When the little girl finally realized that throwing a fit was not going to allow her to get her own way, she began to viciously pinch Anne.

But Anne Sullivan was not easily defeated. Gently but resolutely, she physically forced the child to pick her spoon up from the floor where she had thrown it. Bite by bite, Anne forced Helen to hold the spoon and put food into her mouth. Finally, Helen's rage subsided, and she consented to eat properly, but this was immediately followed by a similar battle over folding her napkin. This second contest of wills between Anne and Helen lasted for another hour. Undefeated but exhausted, Anne went to her bedroom to cry. As she wrote in a letter to a friend, "I suppose I shall have many such battles with the little woman before she learns the only two essential things I can teach her, obedience and love."

Anne was right. Every slight attempt to teach Helen or require anything at all of her resulted in a ferocious battle of wills which the uncompromising teacher could win only through the application of physical force. Disturbed by such scenes but desperate for Helen to receive the help she needed, the family allowed Anne to move with Helen out of the family home and into the small cottage in which the child had been born. "I have thought about it a great deal," Anne now wrote to her friend, "and the more I think, the more certain I am that obedience is the gateway through which knowledge, yes, and love, too, enter the mind of the child."

Anne had planned a system of education which she had intended to follow with Helen, but she found that it would be impossible to implement it. She would have to trust her instincts and wait for an opportunity to present itself. In the meanwhile, her implacable insistence on obedience began to have its effect. Helen became quieter and happier, and although she still did not grasp the significance of the words that Anne spelled to her, she learned a few of them, even trying to teach them to the family dog. In only two weeks her temper was so improved that the two were able to move back in with the rest of the family.

In just a month Anne had taught Helen many things that could occupy her time such as stringing patterns of beads, sewing, knitting, and crocheting. Anne was almost constantly with the child, caring for her, entertaining her, and teaching her. On April 5, 1887, however, in a typical fit of anger, Helen violently smashed the new doll that Anne had given her to the floor, then gleefully reached to feel the broken pieces she had created. Anne patiently led the child outside to the well house. There, she placed one of Helen's hands under the flow of water and patiently spelled the letters W-A-T-E-R into her other palm. Slowly, a vague remembrance of the word "water," which she had known as a toddler, pierced Helen's consciousness. Then suddenly, the relationship between words and objects became as clear to her as the water rushing over her fingers.

Before they reached the house, Anne had to spell the letters for all of the objects encountered on the way. Inside, Helen rushed to the pieces of the doll that she had broken and tried to fit them together. Now she realized what D-O-L-L signified, and for the first time she felt remorse for something that she had done. Language was already beginning to open the doors of meaning for

Helen. By nightfall she had learned 30 new words and showed an awakening affection by kissing her teacher for the very first time.

As Helen's vocabulary swiftly grew, Anne Sullivan was able to give her basic lessons in science, revealing the wonders of the natural world to Helen's expanding imagination. Anne quickly realized that Helen would learn best if she was driven by her enormous curiosity rather than being forced into an arbitrary academic schedule, and their lessons usually took place outside, with small animals or plants clutched in Helen's sensitive fingers. Anne made raised maps and globes to teach Helen about geography and allowed her to build landforms in the muddy banks of the Tennessee River. Helen strung beads as she learned to count and do basic mathematics, at which she was proficient although this pastime was not her favorite. Every lesson was an exploration, and the more that Helen learned, the more questions she began to ask.

There were no tests. Anne's letters to her friend explained, "I am convinced that the time spent by the teacher in digging out of the child what she has put into him, for the sake of satisfying herself that it has taken root, is so much time thrown away." Helen would learn naturally, as opportunities presented themselves.

One such unplanned opportunity occurred one day when Anne helped Helen climb into a tree. Anne left the child to enjoy the shaded perch while she returned to the house to bring their lunch outside. Meanwhile, Helen felt the air turn cool and smelled an approaching thunderstorm. The tree in which she was seated began to quiver with the wind. Terrified, Helen could only cling to the tree and wait until Anne finally returned to help her to the ground. It would be a long time before Helen would climb another tree, a sport that she later came to greatly enjoy.

Nature lessons were much easier for little Helen to understand than the new word that Anne spelled into her hand one day: L-O-V-E. Vainly, Helen tried to guess what this strange word meant. Anne replied to her questions by assuring her that love was not the warmth of the sun nor the sweetness of flowers. After a couple of days had gone by, Anne succeeded in getting the child to understand the significance of the word "think." Suddenly Helen realized that some words described an idea that could not be touched with the hands. Slowly, she became aware of exactly what love meant and what a great part it played in the happiness of her life.

Anne always used full sentences with the child, reasoning that constant repetition would help Helen to learn correct sentence structures and more difficult words—such as pronouns—even if she did not understand them at first. Her success proved that she was right.

Now that Helen could communicate, it was time for her to learn to read. Anne made her paper tags with raised alphabet letters on them and signed the letters into her hands. Incredibly, Anne learned the uppercase and lowercase letters of the alphabet in a single day. Next, Anne placed tags with raised words on them on the things in Helen's room. Soon Helen could label her toys and form simple sentences and was ready to learn how to write with a pencil on paper. To the restless child with such limited sources of entertainment, it seemed like a glorious new game. In fact, Helen spent so much time learning new words, practicing new skills, and constantly counting as far as she was able that people began to worry about her health.

By May of 1887, at almost seven years of age, Helen was able to read her very first storybook in Braille. The realm of books was a greater revelation to Helen than it could ever be to a seeing, hearing child. Books literally formed Helen's conception of the world around her, replacing her silent darkness with all of the treasures of human experience and expression.

Like all children, Helen was soon asking Anne where the puppies, calves, and babies who were born on the Ivy Green homestead came from. Anne was distressed by the questions but answered Helen as honestly as she could, relating what Helen already knew of seeds and plant life to animal biology. Helen's questions about animal life increased when she visited the circus and was permitted to ride on an elephant, feed the baby lions, shake hands with a bear, touch a giraffe, and play with the monkeys.

Helen was also very interested in writing, sending, and receiving letters, perhaps because she knew that Anne frequently wrote letters to her friends. Helen often pretended to write and post letters until the day finally came when she was able to write and receive letters of her own.

Christmas of 1887 brought Helen's first real knowledge of the Christmas spirit. Now the stories, secrets, and anticipations of Christmas were finally hers. Endless gift-guessing games increased her vocabulary, the Christmas tree and festivities brought her wild delight, and for the first time Helen shared childhood's impatience for Christmas morning.

Chapter Three

Learning to Speak

"The place between your comfort zone and your dream is where life takes place."

—Helen Keller

"Wherever she went," Anne Sullivan said of Helen Keller, "she was the center of interest. There is something about her that attracts people. I think it is her joyous interest in everything and everybody."

In May of 1888, Anne accompanied Helen, now nearly eight years old, to Perkins Institute in Boston. Helen was overjoyed to find herself in the midst of children who could freely communicate with her in sign language, though she was also somewhat saddened by this first contact with other blind people. She was nothing but delighted, however, to be given access to the Braille library, where her vocabulary expanded substantially and her love for books grew.

In Boston, Helen's first history lessons took place at Plymouth Rock and Bunker Hill. The child who had no words to give her the gift of imagination only a year before could now picture pilgrims and soldiers, wonder what their worlds were like, and thrill with enjoyment at their stories.

Anne and Helen spent that summer at Cape Cod. Helen had read about the ocean and was eager to experience it for herself. She ran straight into the waves without fear, only to be tumbled underwater in a helpless panic. When she found herself safe again in Anne's arms, however, her first words were one of wondering curiosity, "Who put salt in the water?" Playing on the seashore became one of Helen's greatest pleasures.

In the fall Helen rejoined her family at Fern Quarry, Alabama, where her father went hunting with his friends. It was largely an outdoor life with meals cooked over an open campfire and lazy hours spent riding ponies, rambling through the woods picking flowers, or gathering persimmons and walnuts with Helen's cousins.

One day Anne, Helen, and her sister Mildred became lost in one of their long walks and were forced to cross a railroad bridge to get back to the cottage. Helen experienced no fear as she felt her way from tie to tie; she could not see the deep gorge below. She could feel the rails tremble, however, when a train rushed toward them while they were still in the middle of the bridge, and she understood the danger. Anne quickly helped the two little sisters to climb down onto the cross braces of the bridge, where they clung as the whole bridge trembled under the thunderous speed of the train overhead. Shaken with terror, they climbed back up onto the track and made their way through falling darkness to their worried family.

The year had already been full of revelations for Helen—making friends at Perkins Institute in the spring, discovering the oceanside in the summer, and spending time with family amid the joys of nature in the fall, but winter was to bring yet further epiphanies. For the first time, the Southern girl traveled to the North during the winter and was introduced to a world of snow and ice, where she felt the soft flakes on her cheeks and reveled in the exhilaration of sledding downhill and across a frozen lake.

In October of 1889, Anne began a more organized system of study with Helen, teaching her mathematics, geography, zoology, botany, and reading. Helen was so hungry for knowledge that often Anne had to urge her to take a rest from her studies and academic exercises.

On March 26, 1890, Helen was taken to the Horace Mann School in Boston to be taught to speak naturally. The principal of the school, Miss Sarah Fuller, instructed Helen to use her fingers to feel how the lips and tongue of her teacher moved and how her throat vibrated when she pronounced words. Helen could then imitate these movements and succeed in speaking for herself.

This new skill required months of laborious practice, assisted as always by Anne Sullivan, but it brought great joy and fulfillment to Helen, who had felt trapped by the slow communication of sign language. When she felt discouraged by the difficulties of learning to speak words she could not hear, Helen encouraged herself with the thought that if she could only learn to speak clearly, her little sister Mildred would be able to understand her.

Helen's homecoming was a triumph. The family was overwhelmed with gratitude, pride, and joy to hear Helen speak for herself, a miracle that had long seemed beyond the reach of dreams. When Helen's little brother, Phillip, was born, he would be able to hear Helen's voice tell him how much she loved him.

New achievements brought with them new hazards, however. During Helen's summer at Cape Cod, a friend had apparently read *Birdie and His Fairy Friends* by Margaret Canby to her using sign language. The lovely fairy tale lodged in Helen's mind, and when she determined to write a story on her Braille slate as a birthday present for the principal of Perkins Institute, her composition was a clear plagiarism of the Frost Fairies from Canby's book.

Helen's story, an amazing piece of writing for a child of her age even without considering her disabilities, was proudly published in the Perkins Institute reports before someone discovered that the tale was not original. The little girl was devastated. She claimed that she did not consciously remember the Frost Fairies at all and did not intend to plagiarize Margaret Canby's work. Nevertheless, the principal formed a board of eight people at Perkins Institute to investigate the situation. Young Helen was brought before the board in Boston and questioned exhaustively, leaving her sobbing, humiliated, and hesitant to claim ideas as her own for the rest of her life.

In 1893, Helen and Anne attended the second inauguration of President Grover Cleveland in Washington, D.C., visited the Niagara Falls, and went to the World's Fair in Chicago, where Helen was granted special permission to handle all of the exhibits, and to which she was accompanied by Alexander Graham Bell. In spite of the fact that she could not see or hear the things to which she was being introduced, Helen's imagination was kindled by what her teacher explained to her and by what she could experience with the senses she possessed. Helen felt that she was leaving her childhood behind and entering the real world for the first time.

Chapter Four

Earning Her Bachelor's Degree

"The highest result of education is tolerance."

—Helen Keller

Helen began a more formal system of education in October of 1893. At 13 years of age, she had already studied Greek, Roman, and United States history and could read in the French language. Now she would focus on improving her spoken communication, gaining skills in mathematics, and learning the Latin language under the tutorship of a Mr. Irons in Hulton, Pennsylvania.

The next year, in October of 1894, Helen traveled with Anne to New York City to the Wright-Humason School for the Deaf to continue her studies in lip-reading, mathematics, geography, French, and a new subject—the German language. Helen made her greatest progress in German and geography during the two years she studied at the school, finding mathematics uninteresting although she was quite capable at it.

Helen met the famous author of *Tom Sawyer*, Samuel Clemens, better known by his pen name of Mark Twain, in 1895. "He treated me not as a freak," Helen remembered, "but as a handicapped woman seeking a way to circumvent extraordinary difficulties. The instant I clasped his hand in mine, I knew that he was my friend." Twain was equally impressed with Helen. After their meeting, he wrote a letter to one of the wealthiest people in the United States, Henry Rogers, the philanthropic oil magnate who had given financial assistance to Twain. Mr. Rogers was easily persuaded to take full responsibility for funding Helen's further education, making a significant difference in her opportunities. Helen Keller and Mark Twain would remain friends, continuing to correspond and visit one another for the rest of their lives, drawn together by mutual admiration and shared interests and opinions.

It was time for Helen to be enrolled in a preparatory school in October of 1896. Anne Sullivan would attend all of Helen's classes with her at the Cambridge School for Young Ladies in Massachusetts, signing everything that the instructors said into her hands. Helen took courses in history, mathematics, and English literature as well as studying the German and Latin languages. She did her work on a typewriter. As often as possible, her textbooks were converted into Braille, but when this was not practicable, Anne would have to use sign language to patiently read to Helen everything that was needed.

Helen's social experiences were significantly expanded through dormitory life. In her former schools, Helen's friends had all been either blind or deaf like herself. Now she learned to associate with girls her own age who were not similarly handicapped. In the spring, Helen's little sister Mildred also joined her at Cambridge. When it came time for examinations in the summer of 1897, the principal of the school read each of the tests to Helen using sign language, and she wrote the answers using her typewriter, successfully passing her tests in every subject.

During her next year at the school, Helen was scheduled to study physics, algebra, geometry, astronomy, and Greek as well as Latin. It proved to be very difficult for Helen to visualize the concepts adequately in algebra and geometry, especially since she had never enjoyed studying mathematics.

By November, Helen received Braille textbooks, a Braille typewriter that would enable her to review her own work, and other special tools that made it easier for her to continue with her education. Nonetheless, the principal of the school decided that Helen was overworked and would not be able to proceed with her classes at the same rate as the other girls. Anne Sullivan adamantly disagreed with him, but both Helen and Mildred ultimately withdrew from the school.

Until the summer of 1899, Helen was privately tutored in algebra, geometry, Greek, and Latin by a Mr. Merton Keith. Then it was time for Helen's college entrance exams. Her tests were to be in Braille, but just before the day of the examination Helen discovered that the Braille used for the algebra portion of the test was not based on the same system that she had used in all of her studies. Desperately, Helen tried to learn the new Braille system the night before the examination.

Although the circumstances made her exams excruciatingly difficult and stressful, Helen passed the tests and was offered admittance to Radcliffe College in Massachusetts. At the advice of her friends, however, she continued her studies with Mr. Keith for another year before entering Radcliffe in the fall of 1900, at 20 years of age. She was scheduled to study history, French and German languages, and English literature and composition.

Once again, Anne Sullivan would use sign language to let Helen know what was communicated in her classes and in the textbooks that were not available in Braille. Helen's inability to hear her instructors or read her lesson materials often made her studies much more tedious than those of other girls, but she persevered, taking courses in the Bible, government, economics, Shakespeare, and philosophy, among others.

In 1903, Helen published an autobiography titled *The Story of My Life* in which she described her childhood experiences, the liberation brought to her by Anne Sullivan's teaching, and the hobbies and activities that she was able to enjoy. The vivid anecdotes contained in this autobiography have formed the basis for the numberless children's books about Helen Keller that have been written for a century and more.

The stress of trying to have each chapter of the book ready in time for serial publication in the *Ladies Home Journal* proved to be too much for Helen to handle alone, however. A friend recommended that she seek the assistance of John Macy, an English instructor at Harvard, in organizing the material. Macy was glad to help. "He was a friend, a brother, and an advisor all in one," Helen said.

Helen Keller graduated *cum laude*—with great honor—from Radcliffe in 1904. She had earned her bachelor of arts degree, the first deafblind person to do so.

Neither of Helen's parents were in Massachusetts to see their daughter graduate. Arthur had died suddenly in 1896 when Helen was only 16, and Kate was too ill at the time of the graduation to be able to attend. But Anne Sullivan was there to walk with Helen onto the platform in Sander Theater and stand beside her as she received her diploma.

Chapter Five

Relentless Work and Radical Socialism

"To be without work [is] the heaviest burden a mortal could be called upon to endure. My share of the work may be limited, but the fact that it is work makes it precious."

—Helen Keller

After her graduation, Helen went with Anne to live in an old farmhouse that the two had purchased in Wrentham, Massachusetts. The house sat on seven acres of land and included a dairy that Anne renovated to create a study for Helen. Anne also had a balcony constructed outside Helen's room so that she could safely walk outside whenever she wished.

On May 2, 1905, in the sunny main room of the farmhouse, Anne Sullivan was married to Helen's friend and advisor, John Macy. After returning from their honeymoon, the couple would both live with Helen in the farmhouse. Helen genuinely enjoyed the company of her teacher's husband. She also found John to be of great assistance as she published two more books, *The World I Live In* and *The Song of the Stone Wall*.

Helen's years in the farmhouse with John and Anne were perhaps her happiest. The days seemed idyllic to her, quiet and restful after the hectic stress of college life, yet companionable and filled with enjoyment. Dogs, chickens, and horses were owned as pets at various times. An apple orchard was planted—though it was mostly destroyed by deer. There was a garden for which to care, and John stretched a wire outside so that Helen could find her way to enjoy the woods by herself. Sometimes Anne took Helen for excursions on the tandem bicycle that she had learned to ride, and of course there were books to read.

Helen was certainly not idle, however. On July 13, 1906, the Massachusetts Commission for the Blind was formed, and Helen was appointed as one of its directors. The goal of this board of five individuals was to establish a statewide agency that would provide assistance to blind people.

Helen persuaded the editor of the *Kansas City Star* newspaper to print an article that she wrote exposing the shameful truth about infant blindness. Often blindness in babies was caused during the birthing process through contact with the mother's gonorrhea, a sexually transmitted disease. This blindness could have been avoided if the facts were only admitted and preventative measures taken. A series of Helen's articles on the subject of gonorrhea-caused blindness were also published in the *Ladies Home Journal* in 1907. Anne had always taught Helen to face the truth, and Helen was putting those principles to a practical test.

Next, Helen was asked to write an article on the subject of blindness for the Encyclopedia of Education. The more articles Helen wrote, the more requests for further articles came streaming into the old farmhouse.

As Helen investigated on behalf of the Commission for the Blind and researched in preparation for writing the many articles requested of her, she was horrified to discover that too often blindness could have been prevented. She wrote that she "found that too much of it was traceable to wrong industrial conditions, often caused by the selfishness and greed of employers." Infuriated at the needless suffering, Helen blamed the capitalist system which gave free rein to greedy industrialists. In 1909, Helen Keller became an official and fervent member of the Socialist Party, wholeheartedly embracing the ideals of Karl Marx.

In 1910, Helen resumed her speaking lessons with a private tutor, striving doggedly against a host of difficulties to improve her opportunities and make a difference in her world. Speaking naturally had been a vital goal for Helen since childhood, and it was paramount to her that people be able to readily understand what she articulated.

After painfully hard work, Helen's speech was comprehensible enough that she was able to give various lectures about socialism, civil rights, and the needs of people with disabilities. She attended meetings for the advancement of the blind and deaf and addressed legislatures responsible for making decisions that would affect handicapped people.

Helen also had her defective eyes replaced with glass prosthetics to improve her appearance. These glass eyes were a family secret, unknown to the public, who often commented on the supposed spiritual quality of her beautiful blue eyes.

At the St. Louis Exposition, Helen pled with the crowd for assistance for children who were both deaf and blind. Her audience was so large that someone had to repeat her words loudly in order for everyone to be able to hear, and the response was tremendous. People even pushed enthusiastically forward and grabbed the flowers from Helen's hat as souvenirs. Nonetheless, Helen felt that true social progress was very seldom achieved.

In 1912, Helen spoke out in favor of legalizing birth control, which was against the law in the United States at that time. Helen supported the work of Margaret Sanger, a birth control and abortion proponent. True to her habit of interpreting all types of problems strictly through the ideals of socialism, Helen believed that wealthy industrial capitalists wished poor families to have as many children as possible only for the purpose of increasing the labor pool.

The endless task of answering letters further added to the responsibilities of Helen and her two friends, who could not afford to pay for assistance. It seemed that everyone had a question, a suggestion, or a desperate plea to address to the famous Helen Keller. Often Helen and Anne were exhausted by their round of lecturing and writing.

Helen helped with the housework in the old farmhouse by clearing the table, washing the dishes, making the beds, and otherwise lending a hand however she was able. In spite of weariness and looming responsibilities, she delighted in feeling that she could contribute to the comfort of her friends. Unfortunately, by 1913 the household was facing serious financial troubles. When Anne became severely ill during a lecture tour, Helen finally wrote to accept an annuity which Andrew Carnegie, the immensely wealthy steel magnate, had previously offered to her.

Anne's health and Helen's financial worries were not the only difficult situation the teacher and student had to face. John Macy had announced his intention to leave the household. "He had wearied of the struggle," Helen wrote with regret. "He had many reasons for wishing to go."

Chapter Six

Keller's Secret Engagement

"I am only one, but still I am one. I cannot do everything, but still I can do something; and because I cannot do everything I will not refuse to do the something that I can do."

—Helen Keller

Helen Keller's passion for social reform was unflagging. In 1913, she attended a women's suffrage demonstration in Washington, D.C. to support the right of women to vote. In that same year she published *Out of the Dark: Essays, Letters, and Addresses on Physical and Social Vision* . The book advocated socialism, supported women's rights, and discussed the plight of the disabled.

In a magazine article, Helen explained that she felt the destruction of the capitalist economic structure would do more to relieve the difficulties faced by the blind and deaf than anything else. "This unmoral state of society will continue as long as we live under a system of universal competition for the means of existence," she declaimed. "It must, therefore, be changed, it must be destroyed, and a better, saner, kinder, social order established. Competition must give place to cooperation, and class antagonism to brotherhood."

Helen and Anne were constantly on speaking tours in 1913. Helen missed the freedom and peace of her farmhouse and its seven acres, but she was determined to do her part in advancing the causes in which she so ardently believed. As she traveled, Helen visited many disabled people who were not as privileged as she. "I owed my success partly to the advantages of my birth and environment, and largely to the helpfulness of others," she realized. "I learned that the power to rise in the world is not within the reach of everyone." These reflections deepened Helen's commitment to socialist ideals.

In January of 1914, Helen began a cross-continent speaking tour along with her mother and Anne. Eventually, Helen Keller would speak in every single state of the nation. She was able to hire a secretary named Polly Thomson in October of 1914. Polly would become far more than a secretary, however, taking on whatever duties were necessary to support Helen's needs and goals. Polly was a part of the team.

As Helen traveled and spoke, she became increasingly frustrated as her outspoken opposition to World War I and her avid defense of socialism were marginalized by mainstream media. Everyone loved to hear about her experiences as a blind and deaf person and about how she had triumphed over her disabilities through education, but very few cared to listen to her political opinions. She felt that this was a form of prejudice against the disabled and clearly stated that she was ready to take responsibility for her opinions alongside the rest of the Socialist Party.

Yet in spite of insisting on her own personal value irrespective of her handicaps, Helen briefly supported eugenics and euthanasia in 1915. At that time, she toyed with the idea that it was only reasonable to deny medical care to mentally handicapped babies and allow or even cause them to die. She wrote, "Our puny sentimentalism has caused us to forget that a human life is sacred only when it may be of some use to itself and to the world." Helen advocated that handicapped babies should be brought before a jury of medical doctors who would decide whether or not the child's potential quality of life and usefulness merited it being allowed to live.

In 1916, Helen received the red card as a member of the Industrial Workers of the World (IWW), an international labor union commonly called the Wobblies that supported socialism and anarchism and instigated violent labor strikes across the United States. Helen also wrote an article in 1916 for the National Association for the Advancement of Colored People (NAACP), a civil rights organization for the cause of racial equality.

When Polly Thomson went on vacation that year, Helen hired a young man named Peter Fagan to assist in her speaking tours. Peter was very much in accord with Helen's socialistic viewpoints and soon fell in love with her. In the fall when Helen returned to her farmhouse in Wrentham, Peter went with her. Anne had become ill with pleurisy and needed to rest, but Peter filled in the gap.

When Peter came quietly into Helen's study one day and asked her to marry him, Helen was overwhelmed with joy and readily accepted. At Peter's insistence, however, the two did not tell anyone about their engagement or the marriage license they acquired, rightly fearing the opposition of Helen's family. Nonetheless, Helen was increasingly burdened by this secrecy. She was just on the point of sharing her plans with Anne when Helen's mother heard rumors and demanded to know the truth. Frightened by her mother's display of fierce anger, Helen lied, denying both her love for Peter and their engagement. Helen's mother fired Peter and took Helen away to her own home, where Helen reluctantly and permanently gave up her dreams of romance and marriage.

Helen also had to give up her beloved farmhouse in Wrentham simply because she was no longer financially able to live there. In 1917, Helen Keller, Anne Sullivan Macy, and Polly Thomson moved to Forest Hills, a small, charming, castle-like home on Long Island in New York City.

Helen was well aware of world events. She supported Russia's Bolshevik Revolution in 1917 and listed Vladimir Lenin as one of her personal heroes. She was a proponent of militant socialism and stated that revolution would be necessary to institute a successful socialist system.

Helen also continued to take interest in the plight of the disabled. Up to this time, the Braille system was not standardized across America. Instead, a variety of systems were in use, greatly increasing the difficulty for blind people to acquire books that they could read. Helen herself had been forced to memorize several different systems of reading and writing in order to access educational materials for the blind, and she strongly advocated a standardized system. In 1918, her efforts were realized, and the Braille system was standardized in the United States.

In 1919, Helen traveled to Hollywood to star in a film called *Deliverance* that would depict her own life. Helen enjoyed riding horseback along the trails of Beverly Hills, but she did not find the rigors of acting to be at all to her taste. Furthermore, after representing Helen's story, showing how she could dance, and giving Helen her first airplane ride for the film, the directors concluded that Helen's life story was not dramatic enough to make an exciting movie. Therefore, they supplemented the film with a number of absurd allegorical scenes. The movie would not be a financial success.

Helen went with her friends to attend the opening night of *Deliverance* on August 18, 1919, only to find that the Actor's Equity Union had organized a strike. Helen would not cross the picket line. Instead, she joined the protest march and even went on to speak at the strike meetings in favor of raised wages for actors and actresses.

In January of 1920, Helen became one of the ten founders of the American Civil Liberties Union (ACLU) in order to ensure free speech for individuals who were opposed to World War I, were members of the IWW, or were outspoken socialists.

That winter, Helen, now 40 years of age, joined a vaudeville act along with Anne to raise money to support themselves, appearing on stages in the United States and Canada. First Anne would explain how she had taught

Helen to understand language. Then Helen would come on stage and demonstrate how she could speak for herself and how she could read lips using her hands. Finally, the two would answer audience questions. Many people felt that Helen degraded herself by giving these performances. Anne did not enjoy participating in vaudeville either, although she was a very successful speaker on the stage. Helen, however, loved the excitement of vaudeville life, meeting new people, having their acts described for her, and interacting with the audiences.

While Helen was in a vaudeville act in Los Angeles in 1921, she received word that her mother had died. Helen remembered her mother as a sad, often silent, but very resilient woman, sensitive, sympathetic, and quite capable of managing a Southern homestead. Kate Keller, an intellectual lover of books and nature, had thoroughly disagreed with her daughter's socialist ideas, but she had never ceased to love and support Helen nonetheless.

Chapter Seven

Fight for the Blind

"When one door closes, another opens. But we often look so regretfully upon the closed door that we don't see the one that has opened for us."

—Helen Keller

In 1924, Helen was asked to give lectures to raise money for the newly-formed American Foundation for the Blind. The Foundation hoped to correlate the efforts being made around the nation in order to give more appropriate and effective assistance to blind people in every state. During the next three years, Helen, Anne, and Polly traveled to 123 different cities throughout the United States. They spoke in 249 meetings to a total of over 250,000 people. In addition, they attended receptions for their cause and paid visits to wealthy or influential people who might be able to contribute.

One of Helen's most significant conquests was made at the International Convention of Lions Clubs on June 30, 1925. Helen urged the Lions Club to become "Knights of the Blind," initiating the Lions Clubs' long-lasting focus on aid for the blind.

Helen also had the privilege of presenting the goals of the Foundation to President Calvin Coolidge in the White

House in 1926. She found many generous supporters in Washington, D.C. and around the countryside. One of these philanthropists was John Rockefeller, Jr. Several years earlier Helen had written, "Mr. Rockefeller is a monster of capitalism. He gives charity in the same breath he permits the helpless workmen, their wives and children to be shot down." Now she grandly stated, "Mr. John D. Rockefeller, Jr . . . has made of his millions a weapon to shake ignorance out of its citadel."

Despite her hatred of capitalism, Helen was forced to beg at its gates in order to support her cause. Likewise, she had earlier accepted the generosity of Andrew Carnegie and many others for her own personal support in spite of sternly declaring, "I regard philanthropy as a tragic apology for wrong conditions under which human beings live." Not all of the donations which Helen raised for the American Foundation for the Blind were large ones from wealthy benefactors, however. Everyone from church members to school children gave or sent gifts of money for the Foundation after listening to Helen's eloquent appeals.

In 1927, Helen published another book, originally titled *My Religion* but later revised and renamed *Light in My Darkness*. The book expressed Helen's complete dedication to the social gospel of Emanuel Swedenborg, who viewed Creation as a myth, did not believe in the Trinity, and had claimed to receive further revelations and visions from God that were not included in the Bible. Helen's religious beliefs harmonized closely with her faith in socialism. She believed that the ultimate salvation of the world would be accomplished through practical reforms instituted by human beings.

Helen published *Midstream: My Later Life* in 1929, a second autobiography sharing her experiences since her graduation from Radcliffe. Ultimately Helen's published works would total 12 books as well as countless articles. Her journal and numberless personal letters are also available to the public.

In 1930, Helen, Anne, and Polly visited Scotland (Polly's homeland), Ireland, and England in a trip that lasted for six months. Anne's eyesight, which she had lost as a child and recovered through surgery before becoming Helen's teacher, was becoming worse and worse, much to Helen's dismay. Helen realized that Anne had often strained her defective vision in assisting Helen in her college studies, in writing her books, in reading to her from the daily newspaper, and in a thousand similar tasks. It was a great sorrow to Helen that although she had worked for years to prevent blindness and alleviate the condition of the blind, she could do nothing to stop the deterioration of her beloved teacher's eyesight.

In April of 1931, Helen spoke at the very first World Conference on Work for the Blind, held in New York and attended by delegates from 32 countries around the world. In August of that year, Helen, Anne, and Polly traveled and spoke on behalf of the blind in France and Yugoslavia, where they were guests of King Alexander. Another secretary was hired, Evelyn D. Seide Walter.

In 1932, the friends returned to Scotland and then England, where Helen often made five speeches a day in her efforts to establish schools for the blind in London. After meeting King George and Queen Mary, the three women rented a cottage in Kent, England, for a vacation. Unfortunately, Anne developed a severe and threatening cough. The ladies returned to Scotland in 1933, hoping that Anne's health would be benefited by the fresh air of the highlands. Instead, her vision and health grew worse. By the spring of 1935, Anne had to be admitted to a hospital in New York.

When Anne's condition had stabilized, Helen and Polly rented cottages in the Catskills, Jamaica and finally on the beach in Long Island, trying to provide peace and rest for her. Anne was wild with sorrow over the nearly complete loss of her eyesight.

In October of 1936, Anne went into a coma. She died with Helen's hand in hers on October 20, 1936, at 70 years old of chronic myocarditis and arteriosclerosis. Her funeral was attended by 1,200 people. The grief of Helen need not be described.

Chapter Eight

Late Life and Death

"Life is a daring adventure or nothing at all."

—Helen Keller

Helen and Polly immediately went on another tour of England, Scotland, and France following Anne's death. The two women labored together to read and answer the immense number of sympathy cards and letters that Helen received. Slowly, Helen recovered from her grief and again found interest in her favorite causes of socialism, civil rights, and the disabled, though her homecoming to New York without Anne was difficult.

In 1937, Helen traveled with Polly to Japan, Korea, and Manchuria, meeting with famous individuals and educating people about the needs of the blind and deaf, just as Helen had done with Anne for nearly 50 years. Helen gave 97 lectures in Japan, raising 35 million yen for the cause of the disabled.

Helen met Eleanor Roosevelt in 1938 and made lasting friends with the first lady. Helen was privileged to meet nearly all of the presidents who served the United States during her lifetime as well as many of their wives.

In 1939, the home in New York City was sold. Helen and Polly moved to Arcan Ridge, a colonial house in Connecticut, from which they continued their work.

When the Soviet Union was invaded by Germany in 1941, Helen abruptly abandoned her long-held stance of pacifism. Eager for the United States to ally with the communist nation, Helen suddenly showed great support for World War II and the president she so hugely admired, Franklin D. Roosevelt. In 1943, Helen began visiting soldiers who had been blinded or otherwise disabled on the battlefield, encouraging them that they could find ways to cope with their handicaps and that their lives would still hold meaning. Later she described this as "the crowning experience of my life."

Once World War II had ended and the Cold War had begun, however, Helen's brief feelings of patriotism subsided. A visit to Hiroshima and Nagasaki, targets of the nuclear bombs used by the United States in the war, reaffirmed Helen in her anti-war sentiments, especially causing her to oppose all atomic weapons and warfare.

Helen began a world tour for the American Foundation for the Overseas Blind in 1946. She and Polly would eventually visit a total of thirty-five countries on five continents. In October of that year, their home at Arcan Ridge burned to the ground, along with a draft for a book by Helen about her teacher, Anne Sullivan Macy. It was not until November of the next year, 1947, that a new home very much like the last was ready for their occupancy, but it would take much longer before the book could be rewritten.

Although Helen seemed to have inexhaustible strength and good health, Polly was showing the signs of strain. While on a tour of Japan in 1948, Polly Thomson experienced a stroke. The rest of the tour had to be postponed as Polly's health continued to slowly deteriorate. The women were not able to continue their world tour until the spring of 1950 when they began their journeys through Europe, South Africa, the Middle East, and Latin America.

Helen received the Gold Medal award from the National Institute of Social Sciences and the Legion of Honor medal from France in 1952. These were only two of a countless number of honors that would be heaped on her in her lifetime, which later included an honorary degree from Harvard University.

In 1953, Helen participated in the filming of a documentary about her life, *The Unconquered*, later called *Helen Keller in Her Story*. This movie would be much more successful than the last, but the effort of the undertaking further reduced Polly's health. Even Helen was beginning to feel the effects of old age in her stiffening fingers, but she continued her work on the manuscript for her book about Anne, and in February of 1955 Helen and Polly set off again for India and Japan. *Teacher: Anne Sullivan Macy* was finally published in December of 1955. The following year another tribute to Anne was paid in *The Miracle Worker*, a Broadway play depicting Anne's success in bringing the miracle of language to Helen as a deafblind child.

In 1957, Helen and Polly made a tour of Iceland and Scandinavia. After their return, on September 26, 1957, Polly suffered a second stroke. This time she would not recover enough for further tours. A nurse named Winifred Corbally was hired to live with the two friends and care for Polly, along with their secretary, Evelyn Walter.

The brain damage caused by Polly's stroke left her extremely irritable, paranoid, and unreasonably possessive of Helen, whose life she had shared for over 40 years. The years following Polly's stroke could not have been easy ones, but nonetheless Helen felt shocked and unprepared when it came time to say another final goodbye. Polly Thomson, aged 76, died on March 21, 1960, in Bridgeport, Connecticut. Her ashes were interred at the National Cathedral in Washington, D.C. where Anne Sullivan Macy was already buried.

Bereft of both of the women who had literally held her hands through most of the 80 years of her life, Helen Keller was alone indeed. She could not adequately care for herself or even effectively communicate without a companion. Evelyn Walter, who had functioned as her secretary since 1931, and Winifred Corbally, the nurse hired to care for Polly in 1957, both stepped into the gap just as Polly had when Anne died 24 years before.

It was finally time for Helen Keller to rest. Anne and Polly had both felt the pressure of upholding Helen's image for the public eye. Evelyn and Winifred simply wanted to keep the aging Helen as happy and contented as possible in the years remaining to her. In October of 1961,

Helen began experiencing slight strokes followed by the onset of diabetes. She became confined to a wheelchair and sometimes to her bed.

President Lyndon Johnson awarded Helen Keller the highest civilian honor possible in October of 1964—the Presidential Medal of Freedom. In 1965, Helen tied with her friend Eleanor Roosevelt for a place in the Women's Hall of Fame at the New York World's Fair.

On June 1, 1968, Helen Keller died in her sleep. She was 88 years old. Her ashes would join those of Anne Sullivan Macy and Polly Thomson in Washington, D.C.

Conclusion

The message that Helen Keller's life bequeathed to succeeding generations was not the message Helen herself most deeply wished to leave behind. Helen's passion was for socialism and civil rights, for the creation of a utopia built by the love of humankind, a society that would offer such equal opportunities to all of its citizens that their disabilities could be shrugged aside. But these things are not what Helen's story has come to mean to most of those who remember her.

Instead of pondering her political theories, those who recount the story of Helen Keller today are fascinated by the woman herself, by her complete triumph over adversities so great that she won the attention of the world. Those who draw inspiration from Helen Keller often push past her complexities and her loudly proclaimed ideals. Instead, they identify with her escape from a prison of silent darkness, for in spite of how distant and unimaginable the childhood world of Helen Keller may seem, most of humanity senses the prison bars of seemingly hopeless situations in their own lives.

Helen Keller's life, lived in the dark of blindness, sends a ray of hope and inspiration that has brightened the lives of millions.

Made in the USA
Coppell, TX
25 March 2020